★ IT'S MY STATE! ★

WEST VIRGINIA

Rick Petreycik

Cavendish
Square
New York

Published in 2014 by Cavendish Square Publishing, LLC
303 Park Avenue South, Suite 1247, New York, NY 10010

Website: cavendishsq.com

This publication represents the opinions and views of the authors based on their personal experience, knowledge, and research. The information in this book serves as a general guide only. The authors and publisher have used their best efforts in preparing this book and disclaim liability rising directly or indirectly from the use and application of this book.

CPSIA Compliance Information: Batch #WW14CSQ

All websites were available and accurate when this book was sent to press.

Library of Congress Cataloging-in-Publication Data

Petreycik, Rick.
  West Virginia / Rick Petreycik. — [Second edition].
     pages cm. — (It's my state)
  Includes index.
  ISBN 978-1-62712-224-5 (hardcover) ISBN 978-1-62712-486-7 (paperback) ISBN 978-1-62712-235-1 (ebook)
  1. West Virginia—Juvenile literature. I. Title.

  F241.3.P47 2013
  975.4—dc23

                    2013036660

This edition developed for Cavendish Square Publishing by RJF Publishing LLC (www.RJFpublishing.com)
Series Designer, Second Edition: Tammy West/Westgraphix LLC
Editorial Director: Dean Miller
Editor: Sara Howell
Copy Editor: Cynthia Roby
Art Director: Jeffrey Talbot
Layout Design: Erica Clendening
Production Manager: Jennifer Ryder-Talbot

CONTENTS

A Quick Look at West Virginia 4

1 **The Mountain State** 7
    Plants & Animals 20

2 **From the Beginning**.................... 23
    The Sacred Bowl Game 26
    Important Dates 45

3 **The People**.................... 47
    Famous West Virginians 52
    Calendar of Events 56

4 **How the Government Works**.................... 59
    Branches of Government 61

5 **Making a Living** 65
    Recipe for Blackberry Crumble 68
    Products & Resources 72

State Flag & Seal 75
West Virginia State Map.................... 76
State Song 77
More About West Virginia 78
Index.................... 79

A Quick Look at
WEST VIRGINIA

State Tree: Sugar Maple

The tall sugar maple, which sometimes reaches a height of 80 feet (24 m), is valued for its beauty, its hard wood, and its sweet sap. Every fall, many visitors come to West Virginia to view the sugar maples' magnificently colored foliage. The trees' lumber is used to make sturdy furniture and musical instruments, such as guitars and pianos. Maple syrup comes from the sap of these maple trees.

State Bird: Cardinal

The male cardinal is bright red with a black throat. The female is a sandy brown and black with patches of red on its wings, tail, and crest. The cardinal became the official bird of West Virginia on March 7, 1949.

State Flower: Rhododendron

The rhododendron was chosen as official flower in 1903. Governor George Atkinson, who first suggested the state choose an official flower, once said, "I know none more beautiful and none more common in West Virginia than the rhododendron. It is found along most every vale and hillside and is universally admired for both its beauty and fragrance."

State Animal: Black Bear

This medium-sized bear usually has black or dark brown fur. Black bears have rounded ears, very small eyes, and five strong claws on each paw. They also have a strong sense of smell that helps them find food. West Virginia's black bears live mostly in the eastern mountain region. They like to eat nuts, berries, fruits, acorns, and roots.

State Fruit: Golden Delicious Apple

In 1972, the apple was declared West Virginia's official fruit. However, in 1995 the state got more specific and gave the honor of official fruit to the Golden Delicious apple, which was discovered in Clay County in 1905. Each year, the county holds the Clay County Golden Delicious Festival to celebrate the popular fruit with a parade, pageants, and a baking contest.

State Fish: Brook Trout

One of the reasons the brook trout was chosen as the state fish was because it is the only trout species, or type, native to West Virginia. Brook trout can be found in West Virginia's cool mountain streams. The trout are usually a green to dark brown color and can grow to be nearly 10 inches (25.4 cm) in length.

The Mountain State

West Virginia is located in the southeastern portion of the United States. With a total land area of 24,038 square miles (62,258 sq km), it ranks forty-first in size among the fifty states. From north to south, West Virginia measures about 236 miles (380 km). From east to west it is close to 264 miles (425 km).

If you look at a map of West Virginia, you will see that its shape is unusual. To some, it almost looks like a frog with its two hind legs spread out. The "hind legs" are the two narrow strips of land called panhandles. The Northern Panhandle lies between Ohio and Pennsylvania, while the Eastern Panhandle cuts between Maryland and Virginia.

Much of West Virginia's land is mountainous. In fact, with an average elevation of 1,500 feet (457 m), West Virginia has the highest elevation of any state east of the Mississippi River. For that reason, it has been nicknamed the Mountain State. Some geographers believe that if West Virginia's mountainous regions were flattened out, the area covered would extend well beyond the borders of the entire United States.

Quick Facts

West Virginia's Borders

North	Pennsylvania
	Maryland
South	Virginia
East	Virginia
West	Kentucky
	Ohio

The Allegheny Mountains run about 400 miles (644 km) in length. Several protected areas, such as the Monongahela National Forest, lie within the mountains.

Mountains separate West Virginia's three main land regions. The Appalachian Ridge and Valley region is located east of the Allegheny Mountains. The Allegheny Mountains begin in central Pennsylvania and extend through West Virginia and Maryland. West Virginia's portion of the Allegheny Mountains runs along the state's eastern border with Virginia. These are the tallest mountains in the state. West Virginia's highest point, Spruce Knob, is located among these mountains and rises more than 4,861 feet (1,482 m) above sea level.

The Appalachian Plateau region is located west of the Allegheny Mountains. This region covers about 60 percent of West Virginia's total land area. It is also the state's most densely populated region. This means that there are many people in each measured unit of land. Among the major cities located there are Wheeling, Weirton, and Charleston, the state's capital.

Spruce Knob, West Virginia's highest point, is located in the Monongahela National Forest.

The third West Virginia region includes the Blue Ridge Mountains. This range is located at the eastern tip of West Virginia's Eastern Panhandle. The mountains are part of the Appalachian Mountain chain that extends from Maine all the way down to Alabama. The Shenandoah Mountains are located in this region.

The Shenandoah River flows through West Virginia's Blue Ridge region. The river has deposited rich soil that supports the state's thriving peach and apple orchards. Martinsburg, the state's center of commerce and recreation, is located in this area. Another West Virginia river is the Potomac, which passes alongside Harpers Ferry—a scenic Blue Ridge town that played a major role in the country's history.

Waterways

Besides the Shenandoah and Potomac, there are other major rivers in the state. These include the Kanawha, Elk, Coal, Pocatalico, Little Kanawha, Guyandotte, Tug Fork, Big Sandy, Monongahela, Cheat, Tygart, West Fork, Back Creek, Cacapon, New, and Greenbrier rivers.

Rivers form several boundary lines between West Virginia and neighboring states. The Ohio River separates West Virginia from the state of Ohio. The Tug Fork and Big Sandy rivers define the state's borders with both Virginia and Kentucky. In the north, the Potomac River flows along West Virginia's border with Maryland.

Harpers Ferry is located on the shores of the Potomac and Shenandoah rivers.

Autumn foliage covers the trees in the forests that border the New River Gorge.

West Virginia also has about 70 small lakes and ponds. All of them are man-made. Many of them were formed when dams were built across rivers and other waterways. These dams help control melted snow, rainwater, and overflow from West Virginia's many rivers and streams. The state's largest reservoirs, or man-made lakes, are Summersville Lake and Sutton Lake. Both are located in the central part of the state.

Climate

West Virginia has cold winters and hot summers. However, different regions in the state vary in average temperatures. For example, residents living in the low-lying Appalachian Plateau may have summer temperatures around 87°F (30.5°C). Average temperatures in mountain towns, however, are a little cooler, at around 82°F (27.7°C).

In January, the average low temperature in West Virginia's mountainous areas is 22°F (-5.5°C). In the state's southernmost region, the average January low is 27°F (-2.7°C). Even though the thermometers in West Virginia can hit below the freezing mark, or 32°F (0°C), it is very unusual for winter temperatures to stay below freezing for more than a couple of days.

Charleston, the state's capital, is located on the banks of the Kanawha River.

West Virginia's Eastern Panhandle, which is not too far from the Atlantic Ocean, experiences moderate coastal weather conditions throughout most of the year. Winds blowing in from the Atlantic Ocean help cool the heat in summer. These winds also keep the temperatures from getting too cold in the winter. West Virginia, however, occasionally experiences extreme weather conditions. The temperature soared to a sizzling 112°F (44.4°C) at Moorfield on August 4, 1930, and at Martinsburg on July 10, 1936. At the other extreme, the temperature fell to a bone-numbing -37°F (-38.3°C) at Lewisburg on December 30, 1917.

Many of West Virginia's waterways lead to waterfalls.

In October 2012, West Virginia experienced blizzard conditions when Superstorm Sandy moved through the state. More than 2 feet (0.6 m) of snow fell in some areas and about 265,000 people lost power.

West Virginia gets plenty of precipitation each year. Around 44 inches (112 cm) of water falls on the state as rain, sleet, or snow. Yearly snowfall varies throughout the state. It ranges from 20 inches (51 cm) in the southwest to nearly 100 inches (254 cm) in the mountainous areas. Very little snow falls in the coastal Eastern Panhandle area. At times, West Virginia can have too much precipitation. Flooding near the state's river valleys can be dangerous. In the past, overflowing rivers have destroyed entire West Virginia towns.

Storm clouds gather over the grassy fields of a farm. Heavy rains are common in parts of West Virginia during the year.

This electrical worker clears the snow from power lines in Terra Alta to restore power after Superstorm Sandy moved through the state.

Wildlife

West Virginia is home to a variety of plants and animals. The forests in West Virginia are especially important to the state's wildlife. About 300 years ago, the area that would become West Virginia was covered with thick forests. Over the years, forest fires and logging by humans reduced the number of trees in the region. Today, however, second-growth trees, or trees that have grown after the original forest was cut down, and later-growth trees are plentiful everywhere. In fact, they now cover about 78 percent of the state's total land area. Among these trees are softwoods such as spruce, hemlock, and white pine. Beech, hickory, sugar maple, and yellow birch are also found throughout the state. Hardwoods, such as cherry and oak, thrive in West Virginia. All of these trees provide food or shelter for a number of the state's animals.

Waste from factories and mines has polluted many of West Virginia's waterways, such as Big Wheeling Creek.

The yellow lady's slipper is one of the many plants found in West Virginia. The flowers of the lady's slipper plant often resemble shoes.

Trees are not the only plants that thrive in West Virginia. The Mountain State is also home to more than 200 types of flowering plants and shrubs. These include sawtooth sunflowers, pitcher plants, bog rosemaries, bloodroots, goldenrods, and azaleas.

Black bears, groundhogs, rabbits, raccoons, skunks, squirrels, bobcats, and white-tailed deer are just some of the animals that live on West Virginia land. A variety of birds nest in West Virginia's trees and fly through the state's skies. These include brown thrashers, cardinals, eagles, snipes, falcons, hawks, owls, quails, and scarlet tanagers. Different species of geese, ducks, and other water birds live on or alongside the state's waterways. The waters are also filled with many different types of fish, including walleyes, bass, and trout.

The last century has brought great change to West Virginia's wildlife. As human settlements grew, and towns and cities developed, a lot of wild land was used. Some wildlife species were forced to move to other regions of the state, or out of the state completely. Pollution caused by pesticides and other chemicals used by residents has also hurt West Virginia's wildlife. For example, toxic waste

from the state's mines and steel mills seeped into some of the rivers. This poisoned many of the fish in those waterways. Not only did the fish population decline, but the animals that depended on the fish for food—such as eagles and hawks—no longer had a healthy food source.

Efforts have been made to clean up contaminated water and land. Tough laws and other regulations help to reduce factories' pollution. The hard work of dedicated residents and legislators has also resulted in protection for West Virginia wildlife. Wildlife sanctuaries and preserves help to protect native

A hiker pauses to admire the view from the Dolly Sods Wilderness area.

habitats. Laws have been passed that protect certain animals from hunting or any kind of human interference. Breeding programs and other conservation efforts have also helped some animal populations grow in the state. West Virginians treasure their land and work hard to preserve its natural beauty.

From pollution control to recycling programs, West Virginians of all ages have worked to protect their state's land and water.

Plants & Animals

Sundew

Found in West Virginia's wetlands, such as bogs and marshes, the sundew is a type of carnivorous plant, which means that it eats meat. The sundew has sticky hairs. When insects land on the hairs, they get stuck and eventually die. The sundew digests the insect's body, and uses those nutrients to survive and grow.

Mink

The mink is a member of the weasel family. It is dark brown and often has a white chin and a black-tipped tail. Like most weasels, the mink has a long, slender body and short legs. Mink live along rivers, streams, lakes, and ponds. Food for the mink includes frogs, mice, rats, fish, rabbits, crayfish, and small birds.

Red Fox

The West Virginia woods are home to the red fox. These small mammals are recognizable by their orange-red fur and bushy tails. The red fox eats fruits, berries, and grasses. A red fox will also eat other small animals, such as birds, squirrels, or mice.

Great Horned Owl

The great horned owl gets its name from the tufts of feathers on its head, which look like horns. This owl has a mixture of dark brown, white, and spotted feathers across its body. Its bright, yellow eyes help it hunt for prey, such as small rodents. Great horned owls can grow to be about 1 to 2 feet (0.3–0.6 m) tall, with a wingspan of 3 to 5 feet (1–1.5 m).

Prickly Pear

The prickly pear is a type of cactus. Instead of having leaves like many other plants, the prickly pear has flat, fleshy pads that store water. Prickly pears can be found in the steep rocky slopes and mountain foothills of the Appalachian Ridge and Valley and in the Blue Ridge Mountains. The oblong fruit of the prickly pear is a common food for a variety of West Virginia wildlife.

White-Tailed Deer

The white-tailed deer gets its name from the white coloring under its tail and on its rump. The coats of these graceful animals change with the season. In summer, their red-brown fur blends in with brown tree trunks. The fur becomes a grayish-brown during the gray winter months when tree trunks and grassy areas darken. Young white-tailed deer, called fawns, have reddish-brown fur peppered with white spots that eventually disappear. These spots help them hide among the grass and plants.

From the Beginning

North America's first residents were prehistoric people who came from Asia around 35,000 BC. They had traveled across a frozen land bridge that connected Asia—near present-day Siberia—to the land that is now Alaska. This land bridge eventually disappeared into the ocean. These people were the ancestors of Native Americans. As they traveled across the continent, they hunted animals, such as caribou and deer, and gathered plants to eat, such as berries and other wild fruits.

Around 3000 BC, these natives began to settle in the region that now includes West Virginia. Instead of moving from place to place in search of food, they began to form permanent settlements. The fertile soil was used to grow food, such as beans, corn, and squash. These early settlers also created large earthen mounds. Historians believe these mounds were important for cultural activities such as religious ceremonies. Respected leaders were buried in these mounds, along with weapons and other valued items. Because of these mounds, some historians call these people the Mound Builders.

Mounds built by these cultures can be found throughout North and South America. One of the most famous burial mounds is the Grave Creek Mound in present-day Moundsville, West Virginia. This is a very wide mound that is nearly 70 feet (21 m) tall. It is believed to be the largest cone-shaped burial site in North and South America.

The children of coal miners pose in front of their school in Rock Lick in 1920.

The Delf Norona Museum opened near the Grave Creek Mound in 1978. Visitors can learn more about the culture and daily life of the Mound Builders through exhibits, lectures, and films.

By the end of the sixteenth century, the Mound Builders had disappeared. No one knows exactly why. It is possible that many died from illness or lack of food. The mound-building people might have also moved to other regions or joined other native groups.

At the start of the 1600s, several different native groups settled on the land that would eventually become West Virginia. These included the Cherokee, Shawnee, Delaware, Mingo, Seneca, Iroquois, Tuscarora, Ottawa, and Susquehannock, to name a few. Though they all traveled through the region to hunt for food, many of them also set up permanent settlements. For example, the Shawnee lived in small villages that were made up of round dwellings called wigwams. Besides hunting, the Shawnee also farmed. The Delaware also lived in small villages. These were usually near creeks, streams, and rivers. Their homes were called longhouses and were made of grass and bark.

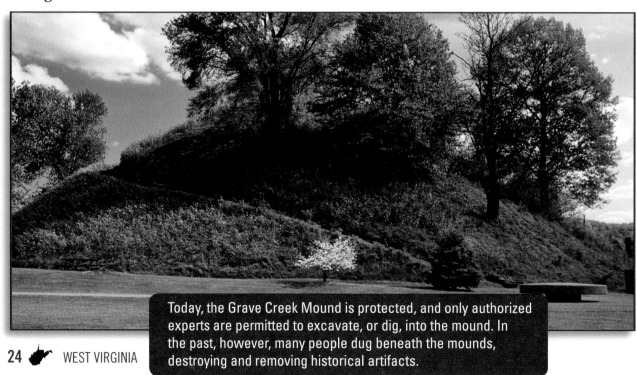

Today, the Grave Creek Mound is protected, and only authorized experts are permitted to excavate, or dig, into the mound. In the past, however, many people dug beneath the mounds, destroying and removing historical artifacts.

Wigwams built by the Shawnee were often covered with bark.

THE SACRED BOWL GAME

Eastern Woodland Native Americans had a hunting range that included the area that is now West Virginia. Some of these native groups competed in the Sacred Bowl Game during winter ceremonies. They used a decorated wooden bowl and peach pits to play. Here is a version you can try.

WHAT YOU NEED:

White paper plate

Shallow plastic bowl or container that can hold the paper plate

Black marker

6 pennies, almonds, or other small items

Bath towel

Divide a paper plate into 4 quarters with the black marker. Use the marker to draw one woodland animal or bird—a fox, eagle, bear, deer, beaver, or wolf, for example—inside each quarter.

Place the paper plate inside the container.

Use the marker to blacken the top half of your almonds, if you are using them.

Fold the bath towel into quarters and place it on the floor where you are going to play.

To play the game, assign each player an animal.

Place the almonds or pennies on the plate in the container. Players take turns gently striking the container on the spot where the towel covers the floor. (You must do this gently and on the towel to keep the nuts or coins in the container, and to protect the container or the floor from damage.)

There are different ways to score the game:

A player scores a point and gets another turn if five of the six almonds turn up on the same (colored or uncolored) side. (If you use coins, you would count how many coins ended up heads or tails.) The winner is the person who first scores ten points.

You can also play the game by giving points based on how many almonds or coins land on the animal that the player chooses at the start of the game.

New Arrivals

In the early 1600s, English colonists began arriving on North America's Atlantic coast. One of the areas the new colonists settled included present-day Virginia. In 1669, a German geographer named John Lederer was hired to explore the land west of the Virginia Colony. That land included present-day West Virginia. It is possible that Lederer was one of the first Europeans to set foot in the region.

Another British expedition, in 1671, traveled across the Appalachian Mountains. The explorers, Thomas Batts and Robert Fallam, explored land near the New River that is now part of southern West Virginia. The area was claimed for Great Britain and was called the Ohio Valley.

This newly discovered land had many fur-bearing animals, such as mink, beaver, and fox. The furs, or pelts, of these animals were often used to make clothing and other accessories for people in Europe and in other colonies. This fur trade encouraged more people to settle in the region.

As explorers from Europe surveyed the region, they usually claimed the land for their home countries.

In this painting, settlers on horseback look to claim land around the hills of the region that would later be known as Moorfield.

British and French settlements in the area changed the lives of the Native Americans living there. Not only was some of their land taken away from them, but agreements and trading between Europeans and Native Americans affected the natives' way of life. Settlers traded guns, kettles, clothing, and other goods in exchange for furs the natives had collected. Many natives adopted the ways of life of the Europeans. In addition, many native groups used the guns and other European weapons against other native groups that did not have the same weaponry.

Further explorations and settlement continued. In the 1720s, settlers from Pennsylvania moved to the region that is now part of West Virginia's Eastern Panhandle. These settlers founded the town of Mecklenburg, which was later called Shepherdstown. Located on the banks of the Potamac River, it is the state's oldest European settlement.

As white settlers began moving into the region, they took over the lands belonging to the Native Americans. As a result, fights often broke out between settlers and natives. To make matters worse, in 1754, the French and the British were fighting in the Ohio Valley. In Europe, France and Great Britain had been warring with each other for decades. That conflict spilled over into North

Today Shepherdstown is home to about 1,736 people.

America and became known as the French and Indian War. It not only involved France and Great Britain, but also their Native American allies, who helped each side in the fight. Forts offered settlers protection from the fighting. Some settlements were actually located within the walls of the forts. For example, Fort Blair protected the city that is now known as Point Pleasant, and Fort Fincastle protected the village of Wheeling.

In 1763, the French and Indian War came to a close. Great Britain, the winner, gained all of France's land east of the Mississippi River. More settlers came to the region. The British attempted to maintain peace with the Native Americans by forbidding settlers from taking any land west of the Appalachian Mountains. Unfortunately, many settlers ignored this and continued to move westward.

A Mingo chief named Logan lived peacefully with the new white pioneers. However, in 1773 a group led by a man named Michael Cresap killed many Shawnee and other Native Americans. In 1774, Cresap's men murdered many

This engraving from 1775 shows one of the battles of the French and Indian War, which was part of a larger conflict called the Seven Years' War.

peaceful Mingo people, including members of Chief Logan's family. Angered by these attacks, Chief Logan joined forces with a Shawnee chief named Cornstalk to fight the settlers. Lord Dunmore, the British governor of the Virginia Colony, sent troops into western Virginia to fight Logan's and Cornstalk's warriors. The conflict became known as Lord Dunmore's War, and ended in 1774 when Dunmore's soldiers defeated the Native Americans at Point Pleasant. After this defeat, many Native American groups were forced to give up all their land claims south of the Ohio River.

In 1775, the colonists began fighting for their independence from the British. During the American Revolution, battles were fought throughout the different colonies. Many of the Native Americans in the Ohio Valley sided with the British. As colonists continued to settle Native American land that had been protected by British treaties, the natives continued to fight the colonists. The British encouraged this, because they hoped to weaken the revolutionary armies.

The lives of pioneers in western Virginia's mountainous regions were very different from the lives of the residents in eastern Virginia.

The American Revolution ended in 1783 with victory for the colonists. A short time afterward, settlers once again began pouring into the area that is now West Virginia. This settlement pushed remaining Native Americans farther west into present-day Indiana. A huge battle took place in 1794 at Fallen Timbers, in present-day northwestern Ohio. About 2,000 Native Americans, including Mingo, Shawnee, Delaware, Ottawa, Miami, and Chippewa warriors, fought against the new US Army led by General Anthony Wayne. The Native Americans did not win, and they eventually signed another treaty that gave up all their remaining claims to western Virginia.

Quick Facts

In 1777, colonial soldiers took Chief Cornstalk as a hostage. He had come in peace to warn a white settlement that the British were trying to convince the Shawnee to attack white settlers. However, the soldiers shot Chief Cornstalk in revenge for an attack by other Native Americans. Cornstalk's murder ended all peaceful relations between the Shawnee and the settlers in the region.

East and West

Residents of eastern and western Virginia did not agree on many things. Western Virginia was made up of frontier farming settlements. Eastern Virginia had bustling cities and large plantations. The plantation owners had a great deal of political power in the state. Residents in western Virginia did not feel they were well-represented in Virginia's government. To make matters worse, only men who were property owners could vote. Many farmers in West Virginia did not make enough money to own their own land, so they could not vote. Attempts were made to settle the differences between the regions. In 1850, all white men in Virginia were given the right to vote, even if they did not own property.

Slavery was another issue that divided the east from the west. Big plantations in the east depended upon slave labor to support their agricultural economy. Westerners did not need slaves to run their small farms, and many thought that slavery was wrong.

This monument marks the location of the Battle of Fallen Timbers.

After the raid on Harpers Ferry, John Brown and his men tried to flee. However, they were captured, brought to trial, and found guilty.

One passionate abolitionist, or person who opposed slavery, was a man named John Brown. He and his followers made history when they raided the town of Harpers Ferry, in the hopes of starting a slave rebellion. United States forces fought back, and many of John Brown's men were killed—including Brown's son. Brown and the rest of his men were captured and tried in court for treason and murder. Brown was hanged in 1859, and six other raiders were also tried, found guilty, and executed. Though the raid on Harpers Ferry did not accomplish what Brown had hoped, it did help other abolitionists' causes. Brown's actions brought more attention to the issue of slavery, angering people on both sides.

A State is Born and Torn Apart

After the publicity that followed John Brown's failed raid, the slavery question grew in everyone's mind. Things began to really change in 1860 when Abraham Lincoln became president. He and his Republican Party were strongly against slavery. They wanted to prevent it from spreading into the new western territories. The southern slaveholders felt the decision on whether to be a free or slave state should be decided by each state, not by the federal government. The idea they supported became known as states' rights. The southern slaveholders were also concerned Lincoln would not only restrict slavery in any new western regions but would also rule against slavery in the southern states.

In 1861 South Carolina voted to secede, or withdraw from, the Union. Soon North Carolina, Georgia, Florida, Arkansas, Tennessee, Alabama, Louisiana, Mississippi, and Texas followed. The Civil War officially began in 1861. President Lincoln called for 75,000 volunteers to fight in the war.

Virginia was still undecided about secession. Although the majority of western Virginian representatives wanted to stay a part of the Union, the state decided to secede on April 17, 1861. The state then joined the other ten southern states to form the Confederacy. Six months later, western Virginians decided they had had enough. They chose to break away from Virginia by a vote of 18,408 to 781. On June 20, 1863, President Lincoln signed a bill that admitted West Virginia as the nation's 35th state.

Unlike its neighbors to the east and south, West Virginia experienced few battles on its soil during the Civil War. A major one, however, did take place on

West Virginia had soldiers on both sides of the Civil War.

A steam engine arrives at a stop in Montgomery, West Virginia. The railroads made shipping goods easier and also brought tourists to the Mountain State.

November 6, 1863, at Droop Mountain. The Union Army easily defeated a large number of Confederate forces. All in all, more than 30,000 West Virginia men volunteered for the Union Army. Not everyone in West Virginia supported the Union, though. In fact, about 7,000 West Virginians fought on the side of the Confederacy.

On February 3, 1865, West Virginia abolished slavery. Two months later, the Civil War finally came to an end when a treaty was signed at the Appomattox Court House near Lynchburg, Virginia.

A famous family feud between the Hatfields and the McCoys has its roots in the Civil War as well as in West Virginia history. The Hatfields of Logan County, West Virginia, sided with the Confederacy. The McCoys, from across the state line in Kentucky, sided with the Union. A bitter shooting war between the two families started when a pig from one family's farm ran away and was killed, cooked, and eaten by the other. Fighting between the two clans lasted several generations and resulted in a number of killings.

Industry

Between its admission into the Union and the early 1870s, agriculture was still an important part of West Virginia's economy. Industry soon became important, too, mostly because of improved technology and transportation.

Up until the early 1870s, West Virginia's many rivers served as the state's primary transportation routes. Rivers were the most efficient way for farmers

The mining companies owned all the housing that was close to the mines. Miners had no choice but to rent their homes from the mining companies.

and merchants to get their goods to market. After the Civil War, dams and locks were built on many of the rivers to help control the rivers' depths and flow. As a result, riverboat pilots could figure out easier and faster ways to haul goods such as produce, timber, clothing, and coal. The locks were designed to release huge quantities of stored water into shallow parts of the river when boats needed to pass through. This greatly increased river traffic and improved trade up and down West Virginia's many rivers. Even with improvements in riverboat transportation, though, there simply were not enough boats to keep up with West Virginia's booming timber and coal production.

A perfect solution came in the form of railroad transportation. In 1873, railroad workers completed the Chesapeake and Ohio Railroad in southern West Virginia. It connected the farmland community of Huntington to large cities on the Atlantic Coast. Other railroad lines were also soon completed.

Coal Becomes King

The coming of the railroads, plus increased industrialization throughout the United States, increased the demand for coal. Coal was used to power the train engines and to keep factories running. Thanks to West Virginia's rich coal deposits, coal mining became the state's leading industry. By the late 1880s, the Mountain State's mines yielded more than 1 million tons (907,000 t) of coal.

Many towns were founded near coal mines. The population grew as many immigrants from Europe came when they heard that coal mining in West Virginia was profitable. Unfortunately, what they had heard about and what they actually discovered to be true were two very different things.

Coal mining companies controlled everything. They managed the mines and owned all the equipment needed for mining. Miners had to pay the mining companies in order to use the tools and live in the housing near the mines. The fees were very high and were often taken out of the miners' pay. As a result, the miners ended up making next to nothing for their hard work in the mines. Men and boys of all ages had to work in the mines to support their families.

Worst of all, the mines were unsafe and the work was extremely dangerous. On December 6, 1907, an explosion at a mine in Monongah killed 361 miners. By then, West Virginia's coal miners were at their breaking point and could take no more. Something had to be done.

Working in West Virginia's coal mines was a very dangerous and tiring job.

Labor Wars

Workers from factories, mills, mines, and other industries banded together in the 1880s to improve their lives. They wanted to fight the large controlling companies for better pay and safer working conditions. The groups that came together were called unions. The union created specifically for miners was called the United Mine Workers of America, or UMWA. The UMWA had been able to successfully organize workers in Pennsylvania, Ohio, Indiana, and Illinois. However, unionization in West Virginia was very hard because the mine owners would not allow union people to recruit miners.

In 1912, miners at Paint Creek and Cabin Creek walked off the job, setting off a strike. A strike is when workers stop working in order to make a demand. Some of the things these miners wanted included the right to organize, better pay, safer working conditions, and a nine-hour workday.

The UMWA is still working for the rights of miners, including these workers who went on strike in 1989 in Pittston, Virginia.

The strike brought much violence to the state. Many miners and mine guards were killed. Many others were arrested and sent to prison. When Henry D. Hatfield became governor of the state, he persuaded the mine owners to guarantee the miners a nine-hour workday and to let them organize a union.

During America's entry into World War I in 1917, the miners and mine owners cooperated with each other. West Virginia was able to provide a lot of coal to meet the country's fuel needs. By 1920, two years after World War I ended, the number of West Virginians who had joined the UMWA had grown to 50,000 workers. Around the same time, there was an increased demand for coal. Mine owners began opening new mines and improving mining methods.

In 1920, the UMWA attempted to organize miners in Logan and Mingo counties. However, the mine owners were determined to stop the unions in those two locations. To prevent unionization of the workers, mine owners drove workers from their company-owned homes. The workers were forced to live in tents to keep their jobs. During the winter of 1920–1921, violence once again broke out. Federal troops came in to maintain order.

However, violence continued into the early spring. On May 19, 1921, Governor E. F. Morgan proclaimed a state of war in Mingo County, which was known as Bloody Mingo. A few months later, about 3,000 miners from Paint Creek and Cabin Creek went to assist their Mingo County brothers. On August 31, 1921, a force of 1,200 state police and others faced a large group of angry miners outside of Logan. The fighting lasted for four days. Miners from Kentucky, Ohio, and northern West Virginia joined in to help the workers. The fighting grew so intense that President Warren G. Harding sent 2,100 federal troops and a group of US Army bomber airplanes to restore order.

Realizing the hopelessness of fighting against the US Army, the miners finally surrendered. Their defeat discouraged further attempts at unionizing the workers. The miners also began to lose confidence in the union itself. As a result, West Virginia's membership in the UMWA dropped from 50,000 in 1920 to a few hundred in 1932. In 1933, things finally changed when federal laws recognized the importance of unions and protected them. West Virginia union organizers were once again back in action, only this time they were much more successful.

During the Great Depression, it was very hard for Americans to maintain their homes and farms. Farmsteads, like these in Randolph County, were often abandoned.

Depression, War, and Hope

While West Virginia was involved in violent labor conflicts, much of the rest of the United States was enjoying a period of economic success. Things came to a screeching halt, however, in 1929 when the stock market crashed. Many people lost their savings and could not pay for their homes. They stopped buying so many goods that many companies that made those goods collapsed. This great slowdown in economic activity eventually brought about the Great Depression.

The Depression hit West Virginia especially hard. Wages in the state were already lower than in other places. With factories producing fewer goods nationwide, less coal was needed. Many of West Virginia's miners lost their jobs. The Great Depression also affected farmers in the state. Many of them ended up losing their land because they could not afford to pay their taxes.

The Great Depression touched almost everyone in the United States. To help provide relief for the suffering country, President Franklin D. Roosevelt created a set of programs that would help put people back to work and rebuild the country. One of his New Deal employment programs that was very successful in West Virginia was the Civilian Conservation Corps, or CCC. This program gave West Virginia residents the opportunity to work in the state's forests. Some of the jobs they accomplished included planting millions of trees, developing state and national parks, fighting forest fires, and creating hiking trails through West Virginia's wilderness. More than $7.5 million was spent on the CCC program in West Virginia. It provided housing for the young workers in the form of more than 60 camps that were set up throughout the state.

Another New Deal program that worked very well in West Virginia was the Federal Emergency Relief Administration, or FERA. Under FERA, more than 60,000 West Virginians were put to work building roads and highways.

On December 7, 1941, the country of Japan attacked the United States at Pearl Harbor, in Hawaii. This attack brought the United States into World War II. The war helped the nation's economy. Fuel, farm products, and other goods were needed for the military troops. Farms, factories, mills, and mines throughout the state were back in business.

This period of productivity did not last long, though. Once the war ended in 1945, West Virginia seemed to stumble while many other states enjoyed post-war prosperity. Coal production fell drastically as more people began to explore

Though they have experienced tough times, West Virginia's factories and plants have provided jobs for state residents for many decades.

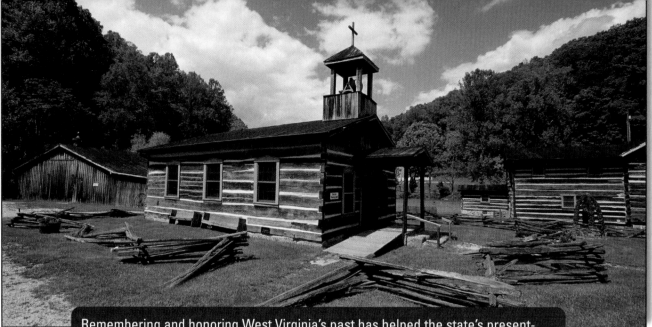

Remembering and honoring West Virginia's past has helped the state's present-day economy. Historical sites, such as the Heritage Farm Museum and Village, in Huntington, help West Virginia's tourism industry.

other forms of energy, such as gas, oil, and electricity. As a result, thousands of miners, once again, lost their jobs.

Disappointed with the constant changes from good times to bad times in the mining business, many people left West Virginia. They went off to search for better opportunities in other states. The state's population dropped in the 1950s and 1960s. Of those who stayed behind, many became unemployed. By the 1980s, West Virginia had the worst unemployment rate in the United States.

Since the 1990s, however, West Virginia has made a comeback. The state government has worked hard to encourage the growth of new businesses and industries. For example, the state government has successfully persuaded computer software companies to move into the state. In addition, the state offered attractive conditions, like low taxes, to encourage the companies to build factories in many West Virginia cities.

Besides the increasing role of the state government in helping the economy, West Virginia's tourism business continues to grow every year. With the unspoiled natural beauty of the state's stunning forests, majestic mountains, and parks—plus the welcoming smiles of its many friendly residents—West Virginia is destined to receive more and more visitors in the years ahead.

Important Dates

★ **12,500 BC** Paleo-Indians enter the region now known as West Virginia's Kanawha River Valley.

★ **1669** John Lederer, a German geographer hired by the governor of Virginia, explores what would become West Virginia.

★ **1671** Explorers Thomas Batts and Robert Fallam reach the New River, which is in present-day southern West Virginia, and claim the surrounding area for England.

★ **1727** German settlers from Pennsylvania establish West Virginia's oldest permanent settlement, now known as Shepherdstown.

★ **1774** Chiefs Logan and Cornstalk are defeated by British forces at the Battle of Point Pleasant. Native American groups are forced to give up all land claims south of the Ohio River.

★ **1859** Abolitionist John Brown leads a raid on Harpers Ferry.

★ **1861** The Civil War begins. Virginia secedes from the Union, despite overwhelming opposition from representatives of western Virginia.

★ **1863** West Virginia separates from Virginia and is admitted into the Union as the 35th state on June 20.

★ **1873** The Chesapeake and Ohio Railroad is completed in southern West Virginia.

★ **1908** The first official service for Mother's Day is held in a church in Grafton. Inspired by West Virginia resident Ann Maria Reeves Jarvis, it is made an official holiday in 1914.

★ **1921** Miners clash with 1,200 state police and 2,100 federal troops at Blair Mountain.

★ **1954** The West Virginia Turnpike is completed and opened for travel.

★ **1992** A law is passed to protect the state's groundwater.

★ **2000** Shepherdstown hosts peace talks between Israel and Syria.

★ **2013** First closed in 2009, caves in the Monongahela National Forest are closed indefinitely to protect endangered bat species.

The People

Today, West Virginia's population is around 1,855,413. Most of these residents live in the state's rural areas. One of the reasons for the state's large rural population is the location of the coal mining industry in the remote mountains. Since the early 1880s, coal has been one of the major contributors to West Virginia's economy. Families whose members worked the coal mines settled in the mountainous areas close to the mines and away from the cities.

West Virginia's cities are on the small side. The four largest cities in West Virginia are Charleston, Huntington, Parkersburg, and Morgantown. Charleston, the state's capital and largest industrial center, has a population of approximately 51,000 people.

Quick Facts

West Virginia's population density in 2010 was 77.1. That means there were about 77 people living in each 1 square mile (2.6 sq km) of the state.

Many cities and towns throughout the state are nestled among West Virginia's hills and mountains.

Charleston is the home of the state government and many profitable industries.

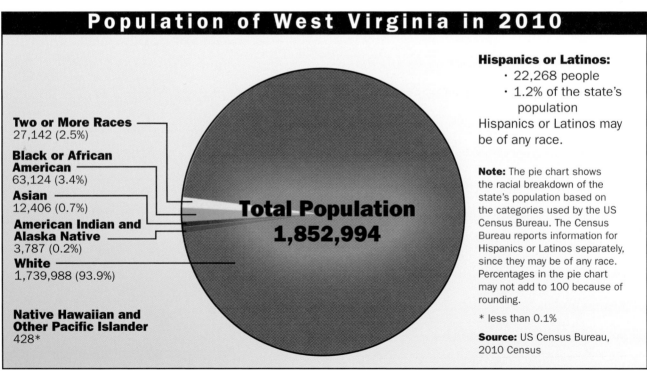

Population of West Virginia in 2010

Two or More Races
27,142 (2.5%)

Black or African American
63,124 (3.4%)

Asian
12,406 (0.7%)

American Indian and Alaska Native
3,787 (0.2%)

White
1,739,988 (93.9%)

Native Hawaiian and Other Pacific Islander
428*

Total Population 1,852,994

Hispanics or Latinos:
· 22,268 people
· 1.2% of the state's population
Hispanics or Latinos may be of any race.

Note: The pie chart shows the racial breakdown of the state's population based on the categories used by the US Census Bureau. The Census Bureau reports information for Hispanics or Latinos separately, since they may be of any race. Percentages in the pie chart may not add to 100 because of rounding.

* less than 0.1%

Source: US Census Bureau, 2010 Census

Lewisburg residents enjoy a food tasting festival. West Virginia has many thriving cities and towns.

This port city is conveniently located at the junction of the Kanawha and Elk rivers. Huntington has a population of about 49,160 people. Another small port city, Huntington is on the Ohio River near the mouth of the Big Sandy River. Huntington has become the Mountain State's main center of trade and transportation.

Parkersburg is located on the Ohio River at the mouth of the Little Kanawha River. It was founded during West Virginia's late nineteenth-century oil boom. Since then it has grown into a major manufacturing center where many goods are produced. The city has a population of about 31,261. The city of Morgantown is the home of West Virginia University. It has a population of about 31,000. Other major cities are the manufacturing and shipping centers of Wheeling, Fairmont, and Clarksburg.

Many events across the state, such as this Italian heritage festival, honor the ethnic heritage of West Virginia's diverse residents.

The mining boom drew many African-Americans families to the state. Some of their descendants still live in West Virginia.

West Virginians

About 94 percent of West Virginians are white. Many of these residents are descendants of European settlers who came to the area hundreds of years ago. Others are related to colonial settlers who came from Virginia, Pennsylvania, New York, New Jersey, Delaware, and Maryland. Around the same time, Pennsylvania settlers of Scotch-Irish and German descent also made their way into the region.

Famous West Virginians

Brad Paisley: Singer and Songwriter

Brad Paisley was born in Glen Dale in 1972. When he was eight years old, his grandfather taught him how to play the guitar, inspiring a deep love of music. Today, Paisley is a country music star. He has won many awards and sold millions of albums around the world.

Booker T. Washington: Educator and Reformer

Born in 1856, Booker T. Washington grew up in Malden, West Virginia, where he worked in the area's coal mines and salt furnaces. He loved to read and learn, and eventually earned a college degree and moved to Alabama. While living there, he founded the Tuskegee Institute, a college dedicated to serving black youth. In addition, he founded the National Negro Business League. He promoted greater cooperation between African Americans and white people. He also wrote a best-selling autobiography, *Up from Slavery*, which was published in 1901.

Mary Lou Retton: Olympic Gymnast

During the 1984 Summer Olympics, 16-year-old Mary Lou Retton from Fairmont, West Virginia, became the center of media and public attention. She won the gold medal for all-around gymnastic performance. She was the first American to win a gold medal in the international competition in 36 years.

Homer Hickam: Engineer and Author

Home Hickam was born in 1943 in Coalwood. Growing up, he had a fascination with building rockets. He and some friends won gold and silver medals at the 1960 National Science Fair with their rocket designs. His autobiographical novel *Rocket Boys* was later turned into the film *October Sky*. Hickam went on to work as an engineer for NASA and write several other books.

Chuck Yeager: Aviation Pioneer

Chuck Yeager, who was born in Myra in 1923, was a World War II fighter pilot who became a test pilot after the war. In 1947, he made history by becoming the first pilot to fly faster than the speed of sound. Writer Tom Wolfe wrote about Yeager and the United States' first astronauts in his book *The Right Stuff*, which was later made into a film. Today, Charleston's airport is named in Chuck Yeager's honor.

Thomas "Stonewall" Jackson: Confederate General

A brilliant military planner, Thomas "Stonewall" Jackson, born in Clarksburg on January 21, 1824, was one of the greatest generals of the Confederacy during the Civil War. His forces defeated the Union Army at the First Battle of Bull Run, where he earned his nickname. The odds were not in Jackson's favor, but he and his men stood strong "like a stone wall." Jackson's last battle was fought at Chancellorsville, where he was accidentally wounded by his own troops. He died a few days later.

At the turn of the twentieth century, immigrants from Ireland, Italy, Poland, and Hungary also arrived in the state seeking work in the growing coal, lumber, and manufacturing industries. Some of the descendants of these later arrivals can still be found today in West Virginia's coal-mining regions and industrial centers. Their rich culture and traditions are very much alive, too. Examples include Lewis County's Irish Spring Festival and Clarksburg's Italian Heritage Festival.

African Americans make up about 3.5 percent of West Virginia's population. Some of these West Virginians have ancestors who entered the state between 1870 and 1930. They came from Kentucky, Pennsylvania, and Tennessee to work in the Mountain State's coal mines. A small percentage of West Virginia's African Americans are also descendants of slaves who once worked in the region's salt and coal mines before the Civil War.

Native American cultural centers in West Virginia keep native traditions alive through programs, such as this art class, that teach younger generations about their heritage.

People of Hispanic or Latino heritage make up about 1.3 percent of the state's population. Asians and Asian Americans represent 0.7 percent of the population. Native Americans, who were once the only people living in the region, make up an even smaller portion of the population at only 0.2 percent. Despite these low numbers, all of these West Virginians—no matter what their background may be—play important roles in the state. Besides sharing their heritage and culture through events around the state, they also play an important role in the state's economy. It is this mixture of history, culture, and industry that helps to make the Mountain State strong.

A father and daughter work in their garden in Frankford. West Virginians of all ages and backgrounds take pride in their state and are proud to be residents of the Mountain State.

Calendar of Events

★ **Gardner Winter Music Festival**

Visitors can get a strong sense of West Virginia's musical heritage at the Gardner Winter Music Festival, held in late February. The festival showcases traditional Appalachian music performed by musicians from West Virginia, Kentucky, Virginia, Pennsylvania, Ohio, and other states.

★ **Irish Spring Festival**

A town in Lewis County, West Virginia, called Ireland, was founded by an Irishman named Andrew Wilson. He lived to be 114 years old. To honor his long life span, as well as the town's Irish heritage, the town holds a weeklong celebration. Events include a "pot o'luck" dinner, costume contests, square dancing, a scavenger hunt, a "lucky charm" horseshoe pitch, a fried potato contest, and plenty of Irish music.

★ **Blue and Gray Reunion**

One of the first battles of the Civil War was fought over Barbour County's Philippi Bridge, which is West Virginia's longest and oldest covered bridge. The 143-foot-(43.5 m) bridge, built in 1852, is still standing. Every June a reenactment of the historical fight takes place there.

★ **Cherry River Festival**

This weeklong festival in Richwood celebrates the city's coal mining history. Events include music performances, craft shows, parades, cherry pie contests, rides, and more.

★ **Italian Heritage Festival**

Every Labor Day weekend, Clarksburg pays tribute to West Virginia's Italian Americans with this fun-filled event, which attracts more than 100,000 visitors each year. The event features authentic Italian food, top-name entertainers, and games for people of all ages.

★ **Leaf Peepers Festival**

This event in Tucker County is held in late September. That is when West Virginia's forests are ablaze with bright autumn colors of orange, red, and yellow. Besides leaf peeping, visitors can check out the area's food and craft fair, live music, and other entertainment.

★ **Fall Children's Festival**

Held at the West Virginia Botanic Garden, this yearly event features nature craft demonstrations, seasonal treats, and a chance for kids to build their own fairy houses.

★ West Virginia Black Walnut Festival

When a West Virginian named Henry Young sold 2 million pounds (907,000 kg) of the region's black walnuts in 1954, the residents of Spencer thought it was a good reason to celebrate. The festival has grown to become a four-day, mid-October event that includes a parade, exhibits, live music, arts and crafts, and other fun-filled activities.

How the Government Works

As in all states, there are different levels of government in West Virginia. The towns and cities have their own local government. Many cities and towns in the Mountain State are led by a mayor or manager and council members. These local governments often handle issues such as zoning or land use.

West Virginia's towns and cities are grouped together—based on their location—to form counties. West Virginia is divided into fifty-five counties. Each county is managed by a county commission. Each county commission is made up of three county commissioners who are elected to serve six-year terms. The commissioners oversee such things as maintaining parks and roads, as well as providing local police protection and library services. Other officials elected within each county include the sheriff, as well as the chief law enforcement officer, prosecuting attorney, tax assessor, circuit clerk, county clerk, and land surveyor. All are elected to serve four-year terms.

On a statewide level, West Virginia is headed by a governor who is elected to a four-year term. The Mountain State also has 34 state senators and 100 delegates. Each senator or delegate represents specific regions, or districts, in the state. The state also has representatives at the national level. Eligible voters elect two senators to serve six-year terms in Washington, D.C., and three members of the House of Representatives to serve two-year terms.

After the previous capitol building burned down, West Virginia's current capitol was finished in 1932.

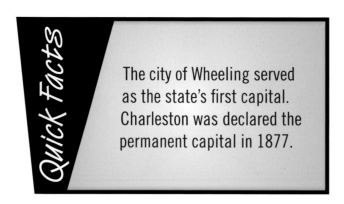

The city of Wheeling served as the state's first capital. Charleston was declared the permanent capital in 1877.

From Bill to Law

West Virginia's elected representatives often write and propose bills in response to the concerns of ordinary citizens. The process follows five principal stages: committee action, floor action, action by the second committee, conference committee action, and action by the governor.

Before a delegate introduces a bill, the clerk of the senate or house identifies the bill with a number. That number is used to refer to the bill throughout the period of consideration. Once the bill is numbered, the president of the senate or the speaker of the house gives the bill to a standing committee. A standing committee is a small group of senators or delegates who are assigned to study bills about specific subjects. For example, a senate standing committee might be made up of senators who are experts in crime control. This process enables more bills to be studied because they go directly to those who are experts in their field.

After the standing committee examines the bill, the committee files a written report. The report will state whether the committee recommends passing the bill—perhaps with amendments, or changes—or rejecting it. Some bills "die in committee." That means the committee members may not have had the time needed to study the bill or that the members may have decided the bill should not be recommended to the other members of the senate or house for action.

If the committee recommends passing the bill, it is then reported to the members of the house or the senate, where it is read three times. During the first reading, the members of the house or senate are simply told that a bill is about

Branches of Government

EXECUTIVE ★ ★ ★ ★ ★ ★ ★ ★

West Virginia's executive branch is charged with making sure that the state's laws are carried out. A governor, who is elected to a four-year term, heads up the executive branch. The governor has the power to veto, or to reject, laws or parts of laws that the state legislature passes. As chief executive of the state, he or she also has the power to prepare a budget, choose department heads, call out the National Guard during emergencies, and other powers. The executive branch also includes the secretary of state, the auditor who supervises the state's finances and budget, and the state attorney general. Like the governor, each is elected to a four-year term.

LEGISLATIVE ★ ★ ★ ★ ★ ★ ★ ★

West Virginia's legislative branch is in charge of making and amending, or changing, the state's laws. The legislature is divided into two houses: the senate and the house of delegates. When both houses agree on a bill, it is sent to the governor for his or her signature. Once the governor signs the bill, it becomes law.

JUDICIAL ★ ★ ★ ★ ★ ★ ★ ★

The judicial branch of West Virginia's state government is responsible for interpreting the laws that the state's legislature passes. West Virginia's highest court is the State Supreme Court of Appeals, which rules on whether laws are in agreement with West Virginia's constitution. The judicial branch also includes circuit, magistrate, and municipal courts.

to be considered. On the second reading, members vote on the amendments suggested by the committee, as well as the amendments individual members of the house or senate may have proposed. Voting on the passage of the bill takes place during the third reading. If a bill passes in one house, it is sent to the other and the process is repeated.

West Virginia's legislators discuss, approve, and reject laws in the State Capitol.

If the second house makes changes to a bill, it is sent back to the other house to see if its members agree. If they do not agree and the second house refuses to remove the changes, a conference committee is called. The conference committee is made up of an equal number of members from each house. Their job is to try to work things out.

If the conference committee reaches a compromise, both houses must adopt its ruling and vote on the bill again. After a bill passes both houses, it is sent to the governor, who either signs the bill into law or vetoes it. If the governor vetoes the bill, the legislature may vote to override the veto. If the legislature then reaches a majority vote in favor of passing the bill, it can override the governor's veto. When that happens, the bill becomes law without the governor's approval.

You Can Make A Difference

Many ideas for laws come from ordinary citizens. It is the job of the state legislators to listen to the residents' concerns and ideas. If you have an issue that you think is important to your state, do not be afraid to talk about it. You can ask your parents, teachers, or media specialists to help you research the issue and how to bring it to the attention of your state legislators. You can make a difference.

Contacting Lawmakers

★ ★ ★ ★ ★ ★ ★ ★ ★ ★ ★ ★

If you are interested in contacting West Virginia's state legislators, go to

http://www.legis.state.wv.us

You can search for legislators and their contact information by name, zip code, or district.

Earl Ray Tomblin became the governor of West Virginia in 2010.

Making a Living

For a state marked with so many resources and much natural beauty, West Virginia has had its share of economic ups and downs. Its once-flourishing coal mining and steel manufacturing industries have suffered downturns as the nation's economy changed. Coal production dropped dramatically after World War II when industries switched to other sources of energy such as gas and oil. As a result, thousands of miners lost their jobs.

Steelworkers were faced with the same problem when demand for steel was drastically reduced. Foreign countries outside of the United States began to offer their steel at cheaper prices throughout the 1980s and into the early 1990s. With this major loss of jobs, many unemployed workers began leaving the state.

Today, West Virginia's mining, manufacturing, and service industries seem to be in better shape. Demand for coal is up. However, to make sure that the state's economy stays healthy, it has become necessary for state governmental officials to attract newer businesses to the state. Thanks to their efforts, numerous computer software companies have moved into an area between Morgantown and Clarksburg. This had led some Mountain State residents to call that region Software Valley.

Quick Facts

In July 2013, West Virginia's unemployment rate was 6.2 percent, which was the fifteenth lowest rate in the nation.

Though the industry has had its ups and downs, mining in West Virginia still remains an important part of the state's economy.

West Virginia's Industries and Workers (June 2013)

Industry	Number of People Working in That Industry	Percentage of Labor Force Working in That Industry
Farming	34,400	4.3%
Mining and Logging	36,500	4.6%
Construction	34,700	4.3%
Manufacturing	49,400	6.2%
Trade, Transportation, and Utilities	135,500	16.9%
Information	9,200	1.2%
Financial Activities	28,000	3.5%
Professional & Business Services	65,400	8.2%
Education & Health Services	125,100	15.6%
Leisure & Hospitality	74,900	9.4%
Other Services	54,700	6.8%
Government	151,000	18.9%
Totals	**798,800**	**99.9%**

Notes: Figures above do not include people in the armed forces. "Professionals" includes people such as doctors and lawyers.

Source: U.S. Bureau of Labor Statistics

The agricultural industry in West Virginia does not represent a large part of the state's economy. There are still many farms located throughout the state, though, and many have been in business for decades.

Many federal government operations have moved from Washington, D.C., to West Virginia. As a result, the Fingerprint Center of the Federal Bureau of Investigation, or FBI, is now a major employer in Clarksburg. In addition, the Computing Center of the Internal Revenue Service or IRS—the government agency that collects income taxes—has opened in Martinsburg.

Agriculture

West Virginia has very little flat land, so it is very difficult to grow crops there. For this reason, agriculture represents only a very small percentage of the state's economy. Despite this, farms cover more than 3 million acres (1.2 million ha) of West Virginia land. That is about one-quarter of the state's total land area. Many of these farms are livestock farms or ranches. They raise sheep, turkeys, chickens, and cattle for meat and dairy products.

Among West Virginia's major cash crops are tobacco, corn, and hay. The Eastern Panhandle region is also well known for its peach and apple orchards. In fact, the Golden Delicious apple was first introduced in the United States by farmers from West Virginia's Eastern Panhandle.

RECIPE FOR BLACKBERRY CRUMBLE

Blackberries have been a favorite among West Virginians since the early days of settlement. Wild blackberries were often picked to make tasty dishes. Later, many residents grew blackberries in their own gardens and yards. Follow this easy recipe to make a tasty blackberry dessert.

WHAT YOU NEED:

2 cups blackberries—either fresh, frozen, or from a can or a jar

2/3 cup sugar

2 tablespoons butter or margarine

3/4 cup all-purpose flour

1/8 teaspoon salt

Have an adult preheat the oven to 350°F (177°C). While the oven is heating, you can put together the ingredients. If the blackberries are fresh, have an adult help you wash them.

In a mixing bowl, combine the sugar and blackberries. Pour this mixture into a baking dish.

In a separate bowl mush the butter or margarine until it is almost creamy. Mix in the flour and salt. Sprinkle this mixture over the blackberries in your baking pan.

Bake the dessert for about 35 to 40 minutes in the oven. When it is done, the crumbly top should be a golden brown.

Have an adult help you take the dessert out of the oven. The dish will be hot! Let the blackberry crumble cool a little before serving it. The warm crumble can be served plain or with a scoop of your favorite ice cream.

Industry

Industry, including mining and manufacturing, makes up a major part of the state's economic profits. The Mountain State's most valuable mineral resource is still coal. West Virginia is the nation's second-leading coal-producing state, just behind Wyoming.

What makes West Virginia's coal valuable is that it causes very little pollution when it is burned. As technology has improved, mining companies have found more efficient ways to mine coal. Unfortunately, in some ways, this improved machinery has made life hard for miners in the state. While the new equipment helps them mine more coal at a faster rate, it also results in the need for fewer miners. Consequently, some of West Virginia's richest coal-mining regions, particularly those in the southern portion of the state, have been hit with high rates of unemployment. The miners are not the only ones who lose their jobs.

Much of West Virginia's coal is transported by large barges that travel up and down the state's rivers.

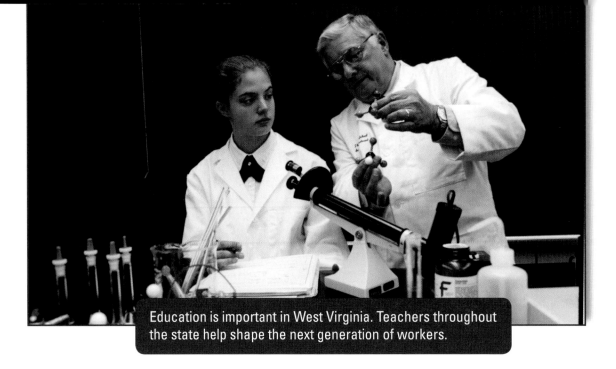

Education is important in West Virginia. Teachers throughout the state help shape the next generation of workers.

People who live and work around the mining communities also suffer when there are fewer people living—and spending money—near the mines.

West Virginia has other valuable natural resources. Natural gas, which is used for energy, is mined in the state. Limestone can be found in West Virginia's rocks. The limestone is collected and used for construction in the state and around the country. Sand and gravel found in the state—much of it taken from the bottom of the Ohio River—are also used in construction. The state's many forests provide wood for the lumber industry. This wood is used to make furniture, construction materials, baseball bats, and other useful goods.

Manufacturing is an important West Virginia industry. Factories in the state make many chemical products. These include paints, plastics, detergents, and dyes. The state's many steel mills also contribute to the manufacturing industry.

Services

More than half of the money that makes up West Virginia's economy comes from the state's service industries. A service industry includes any jobs that provide a service for people instead of making a product that can be sold. Examples of service industry workers include teachers, sales clerks, librarians, insurance agents, doctors, real estate agents, bankers, and tour guides. More than half of the jobs in West Virginia are service jobs.

The most important service industry in the Mountain State is tourism. In 2010, tourists spent more than $4 billion and directly supported about 44,400 jobs. West Virginia has plenty to offer, especially for those who love outdoor activities. During the winter months, the state's breathtaking mountains attract many skiers. White-water rafting is another popular sport, and West Virginia's many fast-flowing rivers give visitors a lot of opportunities. There are also plenty of activities for those who enjoy hiking, camping, boating, fishing, and rock climbing. People who come to do these fun outdoor activities spend money in the state for food, lodging, souvenirs, and sporting equipment.

Visitors are also drawn to the state's many indoor activities. A popular destination is the John Brown Wax Museum in Harpers Ferry. Visitors learn about John Brown's attempt to start a slave rebellion and end slavery. Another popular tourist site is the Oil and Gas Museum, in Parkersburg. The exhibits there feature engines, equipment, and tools used in the early days of the state's

West Virginia's mountains and cliffs draw many experienced rock climbers to the state.

Products & Resources

Coal

Coal has long been identified with West Virginia. In the late 1890s, most people came to the state to work in the coal mines. Though some of the state's mines are no longer in use, many other mines still employ Mountaineers who work in this important industry. Every year, West Virginia's mines produce more than 130 million tons (118 million t) of coal.

Natural Gas

Natural gas is mined and used for energy—for example, to heat homes or provide power for industries. Natural gas is one of the state's most important resources. It is found in the hills of the central and west central regions of the state, and in the upper Ohio and Little Kanawha valleys.

Salt

Salt mining was West Virginia's first important industry. The state's salt deposits are found deep underground, with the richest mines located in Marshall County. West Virginia salt is shipped throughout the country—and the world—to be used to season food or as an ingredient in other products.

Limestone

Millions of years ago, the region that included West Virginia was covered by seas and lakes. Many minerals, such as calcite, collected at the bottom of these bodies of water. When these seas and lakes dried up over time, the rocks that held these minerals were exposed. Limestone comes from rocks that are made from calcite. The limestone is collected and used to build roads and other concrete structures. Most of the state's limestone can be found in eastern West Virginia.

Golden Delicious Apples

West Virginia farmers introduced the Golden Delicious apple in the United States. It has lightly freckled, bright yellow skin on the outside. The inside of this crisp apple is sweet and juicy. The Golden Delicious apple is perfect for cooking, especially in making applesauce and apple juice.

Glassware

Glass comes from crystals and other materials heated to very high temperatures. When it is hot enough, this mixture turns into a thick liquid. Glass objects are made when skilled workers shape the liquid into various forms and designs. West Virginia glassmakers are known for their figurines, sculptures, cups, and stained glass windows.

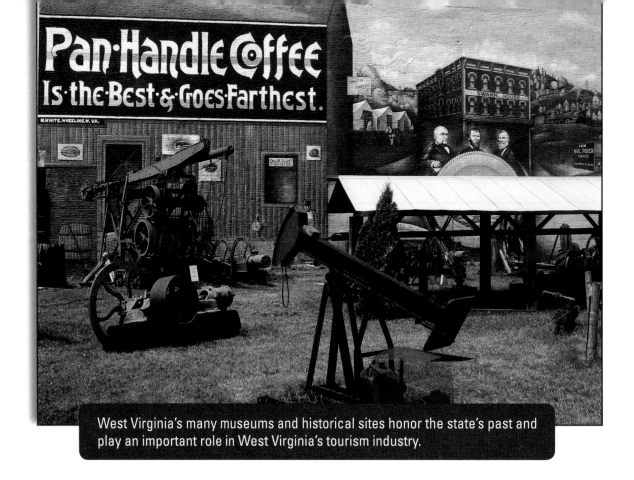

West Virginia's many museums and historical sites honor the state's past and play an important role in West Virginia's tourism industry.

oil and gas industry. West Virginia has other historical sites that attract many people every year. From colonial sites to pioneer villages to Native American culture centers, visitors can come to the state and learn about West Virginia's history.

West Virginia's many restaurants, hotels, and entertainment sites are also an important part of the service industry. Residents and visitors spend money to dine, shop, and enjoy other fun activities in the state's busy cities and towns. Thanks to the efforts of all of West Virginia's hard-working people, the state has faced good times and hard times and come out stronger. It is West Virginians' spirit of dedication, passion, ingenuity, and old-fashioned friendliness that will create a very bright future for the Mountain State in the years ahead.

State Flag & Seal

West Virginia's state flag, adopted in 1929, features the state seal against a white field bordered in blue. Above the seal is a red banner with the words "State of West Virginia" written in black. A horseshoe-like arrangement of rhododendrons, the state flower, surrounds the rest of the seal.

The state seal displays a farmer and a miner. Between them is a large rock draped in ivy. The rock contains the date of West Virginia's admission to the Union. In front of the farmer and miner are two rifles. Below the picture is the phrase "Montani Semper Liberi," which means "Mountaineers are always free," which is the official motto of the state.

West Virginia State Map

Chester

Weirton

Wheeling
70

Moundsville
⭐ *Grave Creek Mound State Historic Site*

Coopers Rock State Forest

250
Morgantown
68

Fairmont
Kingwood

Keyser

522
81
Martinsburg
BLUE RIDGE MTS.
APPALACHIAN MOUNTAINS

Parkersburg

50
Harrisville
Clarksburg
50

220
50
S. Br. Potomac R.

⭐ *Harpers Ferry National Historic Park*

Ohio R.

250
Monongahela National Forest
Smoke Hole Caverns

79
250
219
Buckhannon
Petersburg

Little Kanawha R.

77
33
Elkins
Seneca Caverns
33
Spruce Knob

Point Pleasant
Ravenswood

Cheat Mountain
33

Ripley
33 **119**
SHENANDOAH MT.

35
Sutton
19
250
220

79
National Radio Astromony Observatory

Elk R.
NEW MOUNTAINS
Seneca State Forest

64
Huntington
Charleston
Summersville
219

Madison
Gauley River National Recreation Area
Monongahela National Forest

60
Carnifex Ferry Battlefield State Park
ALLEGHENY MOUNTAINS

Chief Logan State Park
119
77
19
60
Greenbrier

Guyandotte R.
New R.
Lost World Caverns
Lewisburg

Exhibition Coal Mine
64
Beckley
■ *Organ Cave*

Tug Fork R.
52
77

Panther State Forest
219

Bluefield

Legend

- Interstate
- Major Highway
- ---- Appalachian Trail
- ● City or Town
- State Capital
- Highest Point in State
- Mountains
- Historic Site
- National Forest
- State Forest
- State Park
- ■ Other Points of Interest

0 — mi — 50
km — 100

State Song

The West Virginia Hills

Words by Ellen King Music by H. E. Engle

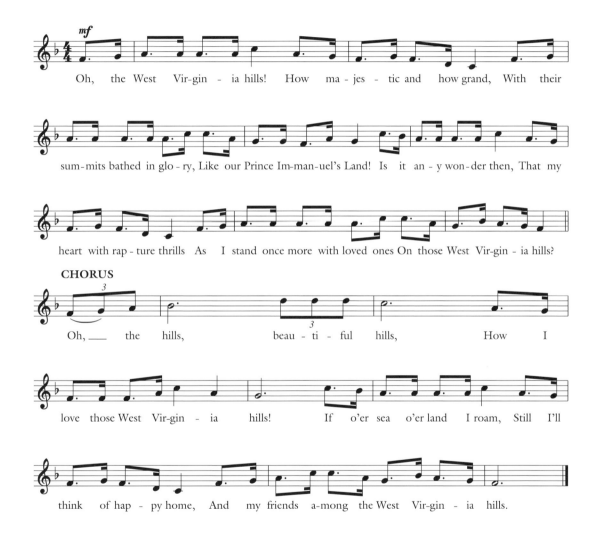

Oh, the West Vir-gin-ia hills! How ma-jes-tic and how grand, With their sum-mits bathed in glo-ry, Like our Prince Im-man-uel's Land! Is it an-y won-der then, That my heart with rap-ture thrills As I stand once more with loved ones On those West Vir-gin-ia hills?

CHORUS

Oh, ___ the hills, beau-ti-ful hills, How I love those West Vir-gin-ia hills! If o'er sea o'er land I roam, Still I'll think of hap-py home, And my friends a-mong the West Vir-gin-ia hills.

BOOKS

Gordon, Nick. *Coal Miner*. Dangerous Jobs. Minneapolis, MN: Torque Books, 2013.

Horn, Geoffrey. *John Brown: Putting Actions Above Words*. Voices for Freedom: Abolitionist Heroes. New York: Crabtree Publishing, 2010.

Somervill, Barbara A. *West Virginia*. From Sea to Shining Sea. Danbury, CT: Children's Press, 2009.

WEBSITES

Official West Virginia State Website
http://www.wv.gov

West Virginia Division of Tourism
http://www.wvtourism.com/default.aspx

West Virginia Legislature Page Program
http://www.legis.state.wv.us/Educational/page_program/page.cfm

Rick Petreycik has written several books for young readers. He has also written articles on history, music, film, travel, health, safety, and business for *American Legacy*, *Rolling Stone*, *Yankee*, *Disney Magazine*, *The Oxford American*, *Profit*, *Performing Songwriter*, *Safety + Health*, and *The Hartford Courant*. He lives in Connecticut with his wife and daughter.

African American, 33–34, 48, 51–52, 54, 71
agriculture, 33, 37, 67
Allegheny Mountains, 8
American Revolution, 31–32
Appalachian Mountains, 8–9, 21, 28, 30, 56
Appalachian Plateau, 8, 12
Asian Americans, 48, 55
Atkinson, George, 4

Big Sandy River, 10, 49
Blue Ridge Mountains, 9, 21
borders, 7–8, 10
brook trout, 5
Brown, John, 34, 45, 71

capitol building, 58–59, 62
Charleston, 8, 12, 47–48, 53, 60
chemicals, 17, 70
Chesapeake and Ohio Railroad, 38, 45
Civil War, 33–36, 38, 45, 53–54
Civilian Conservation Corps (CCC), 42
Clarksburg, 50, 53–54, 56, 65, 67
climate, 12–13
coal, 38–39, 41–43, 47, 52, 54, 56, 65, 69, 72
Confederacy, 35–36, 53
conservation, 18–19
Cresap, Michael, 30
crops, 67

dams, 11, 38
Delf Norona Museum, 24
Dolly Sods Wilderness, 18

explorers, 28–29, 45

factories, 16, 18, 38, 42–44, 70
Fallen Timbers, Ohio, 32–33
farms, 33, 37–38, 42–44, 67
Fingerprint Center, 67
fish, 5, 17–18, 20
flooding, 14
French and Indian War, 30–31

glassware, 73
Golden Delicious apples, 5, 67, 73
goldenrods, 17
Grave Creek Mound, 23–24
Great Depression, 42

Harpers Ferry, 9–10, 33–34, 45, 71
hemlock, 15
Hickam, Homer, 53
hiking, 43, 71
Huntington, 38, 44, 47, 49

insects, 20

Jackson, Thomas "Stonewall," 53
Jarvis, Ann Maria Reeves, 45
John Brown Wax Museum, 71

Kanawha River, 10, 12, 45, 49

lakes, 11, 20, 73
Latinos, 48, 55
Lederer, John, 28, 45
Lewisburg, 13, 49
limestone, 70, 73
Lincoln, Abraham, 34–35
Little Kanawha River, 10, 50, 72
Lord Dunmore's War, 31

manufacturing, 50, 54, 65–66, 69–70
Martinsburg, 9, 13, 67
mills, 18, 40, 43, 70
Mingo County, 41
Mingo Indians, 24, 30, 31, 32
Monongah, 39
Monongahela National Forest, 8–9, 45
Monongahela River, 10
Moorfield, 13, 29
Morgantown, 47, 50, 65
Mound Builders, 23–24
mounds, 23–24
Moundsville, 23

Native Americans, 23–24, 29, 30–32, 45, 48, 54–55, 74
natural gas, 70, 72
New Deal, 42–43
New River, 10–11, 28, 45

Ohio River, 10, 31, 45, 49–50, 70
Ohio Valley, 28–29, 31, 72

Paisley, Brad, 52
panhandles, 7, 9, 13–14, 29, 67
Parkersburg, 47, 50, 71
pollution, 17–19, 69
population density, 47
Potomac River, 9–10
prickly pear, 21

railroads, 36, 38, 45
Retton, Mary Lou, 52
rhododendron, 4, 75
Roosevelt, Franklin D., 42

salt mining, 52, 54, 72
secession, 35, 45
Shawnee Indians, 24–25, 30–32
Shenandoah Mountains, 9
Shenandoah River, 9–10
Shepherdstown, 29–30, 45
slavery, 33–36, 54, 71
Spruce Knob, 8–9
steel, 18, 65, 70
streams, 5, 11, 20, 34
sugar maple, 4, 15
Summersville Lake, 11
sundew, 20
Superstorm Sandy, 14–15
Sutton Lake, 11

Tomblin, Earl Ray, 63

tourism, 36, 44, 71, 74

United Mine Workers of America (UMWA), 40–41

Virginia Colony, 28, 31

Washington, Booker T., 52
Washington, D.C., 59, 67
Weirton, 8
Wheeling, 8, 30, 50, 60
wigwams, 24–25
wildlife, 15, 17–18, 21
World War I, 41
World War II, 43, 53, 65

Yeager, Chuck, 53